Novels for Students, Volume 38

Project Editor: Sara Constantakis Rights Acquisition and Management: Margaret Chamberlain-Gaston, Tracie Richardson Composition: Evi Abou-El-Seoud Manufacturing: Rhonda Dover

Imaging: John Watkins

Product Design: Pamela A. E. Galbreath, Jennifer Wahi Content Conversion: Katrina Coach Product Manager: Meggin Condino © 2012 Gale, Cengage Learning

For product information and technology assistance, contact us at **Gale Customer Support, 1-800-877-4253.**

For permission to use material from this text or product, submit all requests online at **www.cengage.com/permissions**.

Further permissions questions can be emailed to **permissionrequest@cengage.com**   While every effort has been made to ensure the reliability of the information presented in this publication, Gale, a part of Cengage Learning, does not guarantee the accuracy of the data contained herein. Gale accepts no payment for listing; and inclusion in the publication of any organization, agency, institution, publication, service, or individual does not imply endorsement of the editors or publisher. Errors brought to the attention of the publisher and verified to the satisfaction of the publisher will be corrected in future editions.

Gale
27500 Drake Rd.
Farmington Hills, MI, 48331-3535

ISBN-13: 978-1-4144-6701-6
ISBN-10: 1-4144-6701-X
ISSN 1094-3552

This title is also available as an e-book.
ISBN-13: 978-1-4144-7367-3
ISBN-10: 1-4144-7367-2
Contact your Gale, a part of Cengage Learning sales
representative for ordering information.

Printed in Mexico
1 2 3 4 5 6 7 16 15 14 13 12

The Absolutely True Diary of a Part-Time Indian

Sherman Alexie 2007

Introduction

The Absolutely True Diary of a Part-Time Indian (2007) is the seventh book of fiction by Sherman Alexie, probably the most well-known Native American writer of the twenty-first century. It is his first book written specifically for young-adult readers. Based on Alexie's own life, it tells the story of one year in the life of Arnold "Junior" Spirit, a fourteen-year-old boy from the Spokane Indian Reservation in Washington who transfers to the wealthy all-white Reardan High School at the beginning of his freshman year. By choosing Reardan, Junior finds that he is considered both a traitor on the reservation and an outsider at school. His names reflect his internal split: he is called Junior at home and Arnold at school. He is, in his words, only a "part-time Indian," and his challenge is to find his way and his identity through this complex life. The novel is narrated by Junior himself and includes the vulgar language, sexual references, and gritty situations common to adolescent boys. One important feature of the novel is the illustration by Ellen Forney. Junior is a cartoonist, and the novel is sprinkled with his funny and touching drawings of people and events.

The Absolutely True Diary is typical of Alexie's work in its setting—the Spokane Indian Reservation where the author himself grew up—and in its realistic portrayal of the harshness of many Native American lives. The novel won several important awards, including the National Book Award for Young People's Literature and the *Boston Globe-Horn Book* Award for Excellence in Children's Literature in Fiction. It has been published in twelve countries other than the United States. It has also become one of the most frequently challenged books in schools and libraries, as many adults have found the book too crude or too negative for young readers.

Author Biography

Alexie was born on October 7, 1966, in Wellpinit, Washington, a small town on the Spokane Indian Reservation. His father was a member of the Coeur d'Alene tribe, and his mother was Spokane. While Alexie's father, a logger and trucker, was often away from the family, either working or drinking, his mother supported her six children with an office job and part-time sewing.

Alexie was born with hydrocephalus, also known as "water on the brain." After many childhood struggles, including a life-threatening surgery and years of seizures, he largely overcame the condition. Like many children who grow up to be writers, he was an avid reader and serious about his education. Alexie attended schools on the reservation through eighth grade and then asked to be sent to Reardan High School, an all-white school in the small but wealthy town of Reardan, Washington, about twenty miles from Wellpinit. There, he was teased and bullied because of his enlarged head and because he was the only Native American at the school, but he gained some respect by excelling on the basketball court and in the classroom. During Alexie's teen years, one of his older sisters was killed in a fire in her mobile home.

After high school, Alexie attended Gonzaga University for a couple of years, but he began drinking heavily and dropped out. Months later, he decided to start over and enrolled at Washington State University, where he found his way to a poetry workshop and discovered his talent for writing. He graduated in 1991 with a degree in American Studies and published his first book, a collection of poems, *The Business of Fancy Dancing*, the next year. The book received good reviews and more national attention than a first book of poetry typically draws; soon he published two more books of poetry, followed by the story collection *The Lone Ranger and Tonto Fistfight in Heaven* (1993) and the novel *Reservation Blues* (1995). In less than five years, he became the most well-known Native American writer of his generation. He wrote poetry, short stories, novels, essays, and reviews, and his first film, the award-winning *Smoke Signals* (1998), was the first nationally distributed feature film written, directed by, and starring Native Americans.

Alexie has worked throughout his career to find new outlets and new role models for Native American teens. In 2005, he became one of the founders of Longhouse Media, an organization that trains young people to make films. His first book for young readers is *The Absolutely True Diary of a Part-Time Indian* (2007). The book's central character, Arnold "Junior" Spirit, shares many qualities and experiences with the author. The novel won several awards, including the 2007 National Book Award for Young People's Literature.

As of 2011, Alexie has published several books of poetry and fiction and has written and produced three films. He is outspoken against the practice of converting books to electronic formats and does not allow his own books to be made available for electronic readers. He is a popular speaker and reader and also occasionally does stand-up comedy. He lives in Seattle with his wife Diane Tomhave and their two sons.

The Black-Eye-of-the-Month Club —Revenge Is My Middle Name

In the first sentence of *The Absolutely True Diary of a Part-Time Indian*, the first-person narrator names the physical disability that identifies him: "I was born with water on the brain." Later in the first chapter, the narrator, Arnold "Junior" Spirit, describes his many physical abnormalities: he has an enlarged head, he stutters and has a lisp, and he has large hands and feet. He is frequently teased and roughed up, which is why he claims membership in the "Black-Eye-of-the-Month Club." In his free time he is mostly alone, reading or drawing cartoons.

Junior next describes his family. They are desperately poor—so poor that, when Junior's dog Oscar becomes ill, his Dad shoots the dog to end his suffering because they have no money to pay a veterinarian. Junior would like to hate his alcoholic parents for their weakness and their poverty, but actually he loves them and depends on them. He knows that his mother would have liked to go to college and his father would have liked to be a musician, but life on the reservation offers few opportunities for dreamers. He climbs out of his depression over the dog with the help of his best friend Rowdy, the meanest kid on the reservation.

Rowdy encourages Junior to go with him to the Spokane Powwow, an annual celebration, but Junior's fears are realized when he is bullied there by three brothers in their thirties. To revenge his friend, Rowdy waits until the brothers are passed out drunk, then sneaks into their camp and cuts off their braids.

Because Geometry Is Not a Country Somewhere Near France —Rowdy Sings the Blues

Junior's first day of high school arrives, and he is excited about school, especially his geometry class. However, when he opens his textbook he sees "Agnes Adams," his mother's name, written inside and realizes that the reservation school has not had new textbooks in more than thirty years.

Media Adaptations

In frustration, he throws the book and hits his teacher, Mr. P, in the face; he is suspended from school.

A week later, Mr. P comes to Junior's house. He tells Junior that he is ashamed of the way he and other teachers tried, in the earlier days, to "kill the Indian to save the child." He reveals that Mary, Junior's sister who lives in the basement and never goes out, was the smartest student he ever taught and that she had secret dreams of being a romance writer, and he encourages Junior to leave the reservation before he is trapped forever.

Junior asks his parents to let him transfer to Reardan High School, an all-white school in the wealthy town twenty-two miles away. Without hesitating, they agree, although his dad points out that transportation will be a problem. Rowdy does not take the news so well. He screams at Junior, punches him in the face, and storms off. Junior realizes that "my best friend had become my worst enemy."

How to Fight Monsters—Tears of a Clown

On Junior's first day at Reardan, which has an Indian for its mascot, he confirms what he has suspected: he is not like the other kids. They are so white as to seem translucent, and he knows that most of them will be going to college. When he gets to his first class—late—everyone stares at him. He tells Penelope, the most beautiful girl he has ever seen, that his name is Junior, but when the teacher calls him "Arnold" she makes fun of him for not knowing his own name.

The boys at Reardan tease him mercilessly, calling him every anti-Indian name they can think of. Finally, one of the biggest boys, Roger, tells a joke that is racist and vulgar. Junior feels he has no choice but to punch Roger in the face. The boys are shocked; apparently, white boys at Reardan do not settle their differences with hitting.

Junior turns to his grandmother for advice, and she suggests that Roger did not hit Junior back because he respects Junior. Eugene, Junior's dad's best friend, gives him a ride to school one day on his motorcycle and tells Junior that he admires his courage in braving the white school, but Junior's growing confidence does not last. The next time he sees Penelope, she snubs him again.

Halloween—Thanksgiving

On Halloween, both Junior and Penelope dress

as homeless people, and she begins to chat with him in a friendly way, but as fall moves on Junior is lonelier and lonelier. He does not have any friends at school, and back home Rowdy has turned his back on him. One bright moment happens in science class, when the teacher makes fun of Junior's explanation of how petrified wood is formed and Gordy, the class genius, supports Junior's explanation.

However, a low moment follows soon after, when the family discovers that Mary, Junior's sister, has married a man from Montana and left home without warning. Junior's parents are upset, but Junior is secretly glad that Mary has gotten away and gone in search of something better. Slowly, he and Gordy become friends, or at least study partners. Gordy encourages Junior to find joy in books and in cartooning, and Junior comes to understand what he means.

Thanksgiving is another mixed day for Junior. The family meal is delicious and full of laughter, but Rowdy, still angry, does not come over afterward for the traditional pie-eating contest. Junior draws a cartoon of the two of them and takes it over to Rowdy's house, but Rowdy refuses to see him.

Hunger Pains—My Sister Sends Me a Letter

When Junior excuses himself from class one day to use the bathroom, he hears Penelope next door vomiting and learns that she is anorexic. She denies that she has a problem, just as Junior's dad denies his alcoholism, and Junior promises to keep her secret. He also falls in love with her, and the two become a couple, in part so Penelope can annoy her racist and domineering father. Penelope dreams of getting out of Reardan and traveling around the world, but she fears that she will be stuck in her small town forever. One day, Junior sends Rowdy an email from the school computer lab, confessing that he loves a white girl and asking for advice. Rowdy replies, but only with insults.

In December, Junior takes Penelope to the Winter Formal. He cannot afford formal clothes, so he borrows an old polyester suit from his father. He does not have gas money, so he arranges to meet Penelope at the dance. All is going well until the dance ends and Roger suggests they all go out for pancakes. Junior know he cannot pay for his and Penelope's food, but he cannot think of a way to get out of going. He goes along, dreading the moment when he will have to reveal that he is poor, but Roger has guessed, and he slips Junior some money in the restroom. Penelope finds out, and Junior discovers that neither Roger nor Penelope will shun him for his poverty; instead, they are happy to drive him home. Junior realizes, "If you let people into your life a little bit, they can be pretty damn amazing."

While he is building friendships at school, Junior is reminded of his old life. He emails Rowdy again and gets more insults in return, and Mary sends Junior a letter raving about her beautiful home and her struggle to find work.

Reindeer Games

Junior's dad encourages him to try out for basketball, and to Junior's surprise, he makes the varsity team. The coach remembers him as good shooter for the Wellpinit team, and Junior shows his determination when he goes one-on-one against the much bigger Roger and refuses to give up. Reardan's first game of the season is against Wellpinit, and when Junior enters his old gym, everyone in the crowd and on the Wellpinit team goes silent and turns their back to Junior. The only exception is Rowdy, who faces Junior with hatred in his eyes.

During the first period, someone in the crowd throws a quarter at Junior's head, opening up a deep cut. Eugene, who is now an EMT, cleans and stitches the cut so Junior can get back into the game; he tells Junior again how cool he is. Junior goes back on the court, where Rowdy throws an elbow and knocks him unconscious.

Wellpinit wins the game by thirty points, but Junior is not there to see it; he has been taken by ambulance to the hospital. Later, the coach stops by the hospital to check on Junior, to apologize for putting him into the game at all, and to say that he respects Junior's commitment. Junior is not supposed to sleep because of his head injury, so he and the coach sit up all night telling stories.

And a Partridge in a Pear Tree— Wake

As he has done on many Christmases before, Junior's dad takes the family's meager savings and disappears for several days, drunk. When he returns, Junior is hurt, but he loves his dad and tells him it is all right. Mary sends Junior several postcards of Montana, revealing that she still cannot find a job but that she has begun writing a book. Junior thinks about his family and how they show their love and realizes that many of his white friends have more money and security but also have parents who ignore them.

Junior's grandmother, he says, is the best thing about Wellpinit. She is smart and loves to travel, and Junior finds that she is more tolerant of different kinds of people than other Indians he knows. She has no patience with homophobia, for example, and she makes friends with homeless people whenever she goes to Seattle. She loves to attend powwows, where she could meet new people from far away. Suddenly, however, she is dead, killed by a drunk driver while walking home. Her last wish is that the family should forgive the driver.

At her funeral, thousands of people come, and none of them treat Junior unkindly. Mary is not able to be there, but the rest of the extended family gathers and mourns. Into the gathering comes a white man, Billionaire Ted; he is "yet another white guy who showed up on the rez because he loved Indian people SOOOOOOOO much." Ted explains that he collects Indian artifacts and that for several years he has owned a beaded powwow dance outfit. At great expense, he has hired an expert to research the outfit, and the expert has traced the dress to the Spokane people and to Grandmother Spirit herself. Billionaire Ted has come to give the dress back, but none of the crowd recognizes the style of beadwork, and Grandmother Spirit was never a powwow dancer, so Junior's mother hands the dress back. Ted leaves, followed by the laughter of the crowd.

Valentine Heart—My Final Freshman Year Report Card

More sadness comes. Eugene is shot in the face and killed by a friend when the two men, both drunk, quarrel over the last drink from a bottle of wine. Junior blames himself for the deaths, becomes more and more depressed, and starts missing school. When he returns, one of his teachers makes a sarcastic comment about his attendance. Gordy stands up, slams his book down on the desk, and walks out, followed by all of the other students in the class. Junior has friends.

Junior becomes the best shooter on the basketball team but never becomes comfortable playing. In fact, he throws up before every game. When Reardan faces Wellpinit again, Junior is determined to win. Rowdy is assigned to guard Junior, and for the first time, Junior leaps higher than Rowdy and steals the ball out of his hands. He outscores Rowdy throughout the game, and the

Reardan team wins easily. However, as Junior watches his old Wellpinit classmates after the game, he realizes that, for many of them, basketball is all they have. None of them will go to college, many of them had no breakfast that morning, and most of them have alcoholic parents. Winning the game seems less glorious now, but when Junior and Rowdy exchange their next emails, Rowdy's insults seem less angry, and Junior is hopeful.

The hopefulness does not last. Junior is called out of class one day, and the school counselor awkwardly tells him that Mary has died. Apparently, she and her new husband had a party in their trailer. A fire started, and Mary was drunk and passed out; she never realized the trailer was on fire. Junior thinks that if he had never left for Reardan, Mary would never have left for Montana; he feels responsible for her death. After Mary's funeral, Junior runs into Rowdy, who has been watching from a distance. Rowdy also blames Junior for Mary's death, and he tells Junior, "I hate you!" before running away. At school, the white kids hug Junior and slip him notes of sympathy.

Remembering—Talking about Turtles

Junior and his parents take a picnic lunch and Dad's saxophone and go to the cemetery to clean the family graves. They hug and express their love, and Junior finds himself crying for all the missed opportunities and all of the lonely people in the world. He realizes that he is going to be all right and thinks of those—including Rowdy—who will never reach their dreams. He remembers a day when he and Rowdy were ten and they climbed the biggest tree on the reservation. They were able to see their whole world from the top, and it was beautiful.

School ends, and Junior sits at home alone. Then Rowdy shows up. They trade insults, shoot some hoops, and talk about the future.

Billionaire Ted

Billionaire Ted is a wealthy white man from Montana who appears at Grandmother Spirit's funeral. He is typical of a kind of white person who is fascinated by Indians and full of misinformation about them; these fanatics become a target for mockery by Indians who see, as the white people themselves do not, that this fascination is superficial and condescending. Billionaire Ted has come to return a beaded dress that he believes once belonged to Grandmother Spirit, but the research that he has paid for turns out to be worthless. Junior's Mom examines the dress and rejects it, and Billionaire Ted drives away while two thousand Indians laugh.

Coach

"Coach" is the only name Junior ever gives for the man who coaches the Reardan High School basketball team. Coach seems to have no racist leanings; he wants the best players on his team and treats Junior the same way he treats the others. Coach understands young men: he knows what Junior is up against as the only Indian student at Reardan and what it means to Junior to be at odds with Rowdy. When Junior is hospitalized after Rowdy knocks him unconscious during the first Reardan-Wellpinit basketball game, Coach comes to see him in the hospital to apologize for putting Junior in the game and for putting him in an untenable situation. He stays the whole night talking with Junior, but Junior does not narrate any details about their conversation because "that night belongs to just me and my coach."

Dad

Junior's dad, Arnold Spirit, Sr., is an alcoholic, discouraged that he was not able to have the musical career he dreamed of. He spends most of his time drinking or watching television alone. Sometimes Junior joins him, but the two sit and watch without speaking. Although Dad is frequently angry and depressed, he does not beat his children, as Rowdy's father does, and he never misses one of Junior's basketball games. Still, he cannot support his family, and in the beginning of the book, Dad shoots Junior's sick dog because the family cannot afford to take him to the veterinarian. When Junior transfers to Reardan, Dad drives him to and from school—when he remembers and when he has enough money for gas. At the end of the novel, after Mary has died, Dad tells Junior that he loves him. Junior is pleased to hear it, although he has never doubted that it was true.

Eugene

Junior's dad's best friend, Eugene, rides around the reservation on a 1946 Indian Chief Loadmaster motorcycle. Like many of the adults on the reservation, Eugene is an alcoholic, but he is kind to Junior. He gives Junior a ride to school on his motorcycle and, after he has had some EMT training, stitches up Junior's cut face during a basketball game. Eugene dies when he is shot in the face by a good friend; both drunk, they are fighting over the last swig of alcohol in a bottle.

Gordy

Gordy is a student at Reardan High School. Like Junior, he is a bookish nerd who does not fit in. Gordy supports Junior when the science teacher at Reardan is mocking him for his explanation of how petrified wood is formed, but he explains later that he has not spoken up to help Junior. "I did it for science," he says. Gordy and Junior form a distant friendship, spending time together studying in the library. Gordy speaks with a vocabulary and a wisdom beyond his years, and he helps Junior see better ways to learn. After Grandmother Spirit is killed and Junior misses several days of school, Gordy leads his classmates in walking out of social studies to protest the teacher's unkind remarks to Junior, and Junior realizes that his white classmates have become friends.

Junior

Fourteen-year-old Junior, whose given name is Arnold Spirit, is the novel's main character. He is an Indian living with his alcoholic parents and his depressed sister on the Spokane Indian Reservation.

Because he is small and nerdy, because he stutters and has a lisp, and because hydrocephalus has given him an enlarged head, he is a constant target of bullying and teasing. His only friend is Rowdy, an angry bully himself who has always stuck up for Junior.

Junior, who is most expressive when he is drawing cartoons, feels that his life is depressing and hopeless, but the feelings are crystallized when he discovers, on his first day of geometry class, that his reservation school has been using the same textbooks since his mother was a student there. His resulting outburst leads his teacher to urge Junior to leave the reservation and try to get a better education somewhere else before it is too late.

Junior transfers to Reardan High School in a small, all-white, wealthy town nearby, and soon discovers that he is smarter than he thought he was and a better basketball player. At first an outcast, he gradually wins the respect and friendship of his classmates, who can see that he does not give up easily when things go against him. Junior knows that doing well at Reardan is his only chance to escape the reservation, his only chance to realize his dreams though his parents never realized theirs. He does his best to keep his new friends from discovering how poor his family is, and he works hard at school and at basketball. But he sees that he is at best only a "part-time Indian"; at school, where everyone calls him "Arnold," he will always be thought of as Indian, and therefore as different, while on the reservation, where he is known as

"Junior," his decision to attend Reardan is seen as a betrayal, as an attempt to be white.

As he moves through his freshman year of high school and faces the rejection of his best friend and three devastating deaths, Junior learns how to accept himself as an individual with strengths and weaknesses rather than as a representative of a group or tribe. He begins to see the limitations that held back his parents and his sister and that will hold back Rowdy, and even as Junior and Rowdy resume their old friendship at the end of the novel, the reader knows that one day Junior will leave Rowdy behind.

Mom

Junior's mom's real name is Agnes Adams Spirit, but Junior, the narrator, always refers to her as "Mom." She is a recovering alcoholic and poor, but she is very smart, an avid reader with a good memory. Junior thinks she might have become a community college teacher "if somebody had paid attention to [her] dreams" and she had been able to go to college. Indirectly, she is the reason Junior transfers to Reardan High School. On the first day of geometry class, Junior finds her name, "Agnes Adams," written in his textbook and realizes that the school in Wellpinit is so ill-equipped that even the textbooks are at least thirty years old. Mom does not hesitate when Junior says he wants to transfer to the all-white school; she knows that getting off the reservation will be his only chance of realizing his dreams.

Mr. P

Mr. P is the white geometry teacher at Wellpinit High School on the reservation; he is eccentric and forgetful and has been teaching on the reservation for decades. Junior neither respects nor trusts him, seeing him as merely a white do-gooder who has been foisted on the school because no one really cares about the quality of Indian kids' education. After Junior throws a book at Mr. P one day in class and is suspended, Mr. P drives out to Junior's house to advise him to leave the reservation and look for a better education in Reardan. He confesses that, in his early days of teaching on the reservation, he harmed children by trying to force them to give up their culture. He reveals that he knew Junior's sister Mary, the smartest student he ever taught, and that she had secret dreams of being a writer. The reservation makes people give up, Mr. P says, and if Junior does not leave he will eventually give up, too.

Penelope

Penelope is a pretty, smart, and popular white girl with beautiful blue eyes. Junior meets her on his first day at Reardan High School, when she chats with him and then turns against him, making fun of him because he gives his name as "Junior" while the teachers call him "Arnold." For weeks she is cold and mean to him, but she warms up to him when

Junior discovers but keeps the secret that she is anorexic. Junior and Penelope become something of a couple. Penelope never really loves Junior, but she likes him, and she knows that it irritates her father to see her dating an Indian. Penelope is deeply unhappy, believing that she will never escape her small town and see the world. When Junior and Penelope go to the Winter Formal together, Penelope discovers the depth of Junior's poverty and accepts it as he accepts her anorexia.

Roger

Roger, sometimes called Roger the Giant, is a big young man, a member of the Reardan varsity basketball team. In the beginning, he teases Junior with racial slurs, until the day he tells a joke that is so racist and infuriating that Junior punches him in the face. From then on, Roger leaves him alone. During basketball tryouts, Junior is paired with the much bigger Roger in a one-on-one game; Junior's determination to keep playing after he is knocked down wins the respect of Roger and the coach. Soon, Roger becomes something of a big brother to Junior, as he is to Penelope, and he slips Junior some money after the dance when he realizes Junior does not have any.

Rowdy

Rowdy is Junior's best friend, born only two hours after Junior on November 5, 1992. He was born screaming and seems to have been angry ever since. Rowdy's family is as poor as Junior's, but Rowdy's father is also physically abusive, and Rowdy frequently comes to school with bruises. He is a bully and frequently gets into fights with the other boys, but he is always ready to defend Junior against other bullies. The two boys have a strong bond, which they typically demonstrate by insulting each other, wrestling, and acting indifferent.

When Junior decides to leave the reservation for school, Rowdy takes the decision as personal rejection and turns his anger and jealousy toward Junior. He refuses to have any contact with Junior and does not even come by for his traditional pumpkin pie at Thanksgiving. During the first basketball game between Wellpinit and Reardan, held on the reservation, Rowdy knocks Junior unconscious and puts him in the hospital on the way to soundly defeating the Reardan team. His anger is amplified when Junior helps defeat Wellpinit in a second basketball game, and Junior realizes that for Rowdy and the other boys stuck on the reservation, winning at basketball is one of few ways to gain attention and pride.

At the end of the novel, Rowdy shows up at Junior's house. Neither boy says anything warm or sentimental (Rowdy says that he has come by only because he is bored), but it appears that they will spend at least summer vacation as friends again.

Agnes Adams Spirit

See Mom

Arnold Spirit, Jr.

See Junior

Arnold Spirit, Sr.

See Dad

Grandmother Spirit

Junior's maternal grandmother is a tough and sensible woman who gives Junior advice about how to deal with other men. A widow, she wears bandannas, goes to garage sales, and makes delicious salmon mush. She is open-hearted, arguing that homophobia is wrong and making friends with homeless people when she visits the big city. When she is fatally hit by a drunk driver, her last request is that the family forgive the driver, rather than seek revenge.

Mary Spirit

Mary is Junior's older sister. She is smart and funny and tough, and she never lets her family know that she used to read romance novels all day long and dreamed of writing them herself. After graduating high school, she seems to collapse, perhaps realizing that her future offers few options. She lives in her parents' basement for seven years, never goes out, and rarely speaks, and the family nicknames her "Mary Runs Away."

One day, she actually runs away without warning; she marries a young man she met in the casino and moves with him to the Flathead Reservation in Montana. Occasionally she sends postcards to Junior, describing her beautiful life. In fact, she is living in a trailer and struggling, unable to find a job but using the time to try to write an autobiography. During Junior's first year at Reardan, she is killed when her trailer catches fire. Passed out drunk, she never wakes up.

Identity

The central question facing Junior, the protagonist in *The Absolutely True Diary of a Part-Time Indian*, is over his identity: Who is he? Does he have to turn his back on being an Indian in order to have the kind of life he dreams of? From the beginning, Junior is not the kind of kid who fits in. He has an enlarged head, large hands and feet, a stammer and a lisp, and even on the reservation he is constantly teased and beaten up. Although he has never been accepted on the reservation, he is rejected in a more profound way once he transfers to Reardan, the white high school.

Topics for Further Study

- Watch the movie *Smoke Signals* (1998), for which Sherman Alexie wrote the screenplay, and read the short story "This Is What It Means to Say Phoenix, Arizona," from Alexie's collection *The Lone Ranger and Tonto Fistfight in Heaven* (1993). Is it possible to imagine Thomas Builds-the-Fire and Victor Joseph as the adult versions of Junior and Rowdy? What do the younger and older characters have in common, and how are they different? Write a paper in which you predict what happens to Junior and Rowdy several years after *The Absolutely True Diary* ends, drawing on Thomas Builds-the-Fire and Victor Joseph as appropriate. If you wish, write an illustrated "Epilogue" to the novel instead, setting it ten or more years in the future and echoing the narrator's voice.

- Research the history and development of the Spokane Indian Reservation, and prepare a digital presentation for your class including maps, important dates, and statistics. Be sure to point out the locations of Wellpinit and Reardan, a description of the Spokane Powwow, and any other information that helps readers understand the references in the novel.

- Research the controversy over Indian mascots for school athletic teams, and decide for yourself whether you think they are respectful or disrespectful. If possible, contact the administrations of several of these schools (for example, the University of Louisiana at Monroe) and ask about the financial implications of these changes. Prepare a Power-Point presentation of typical mascots and fans, possibly incorporating videos if appropriate, to persuade your classmates to accept your position.

- *The Lone Ranger*, a popular television show from 1949 to 1957, featured the Lone Ranger himself (a masked hero who rode into town to do good deeds) and his Indian companion, Tonto. Out of more than two hundred episodes made, seventy-eight are available on DVD and about a dozen can be watched for free at hulu.com. Watch an episode of the show, perhaps with your class. Write a character analysis of Tonto, making note of any stereotypes you find.

- Read Sandra Cisneros's short novel, *The House on Mango Street* (1984), about a Latina girl who dreams of escaping her impoverished Chicago neighborhood. Write a paper in which you compare Junior's dreams and struggles with those of Esperanza Cordero, and bring in other characters—or real people— you may know who dream of leaving home (you might include Jay Gatsby, Jane Eyre, or even Luke Skywalker). Is the experience different for boys and for girls? For Indians and for Latinas? For modern people and those living in the past? What can you generalize about the need to leave home and make one's own way?

- Choose one of the chapters in *The Absolutely True Diary of a Part-Time Indian* that is not illustrated, and create a cartoon for it in the style of those in the book.

- Prepare a short video or podcast of tips for students who will soon spend their first day at your school. Use humor to give advice and to point out common mistakes that new students sometimes make. Ask permission from your principal to post it on You-Tube or show it on your school news station.

When he tells Rowdy, his only friend, that he is transferring, Rowdy punches him in the face and shouts, "You always thought you were better than me." In the drawing Junior makes after the argument, Rowdy is calling Junior a "white lover." When Reardan plays basketball at Wellpinit, the reservation crowd taunts Junior by shouting the name he is called at Reardan, "Arnold," and turns away from him. In their minds, he is no longer an Indian.

However, Junior knows that he does not belong at Reardan, either. "I woke up on the reservation as an Indian," he says, "and somewhere on the road to Reardan I became something less than Indian." For the first several weeks, no one at school will even speak to him. Once he has made a few friends and begun to fit in with the white students, his identity becomes even more confusing. He notes, "Traveling between Reardan and Wellpinit … I always felt like a stranger. I was half Indian in one place and half white in the other."

Junior's learning to shape his two lives into a coherent whole is the major theme of the novel. He has to learn to cherish the traditions and strengths of his native culture while rejecting the weaknesses, including hopelessness and alcoholism, and he must incorporate values that are seen as "white," including a new way of thinking about education. In the end, Junior realizes that he belongs to many groups: "I was a Spokane Indian. I belonged to that tribe. But I also belonged to the tribe of American immigrants. And to the tribe of basketball players.

And to the tribe of bookworms." Junior claims membership in fourteen tribes, and concludes, "That's when I knew that I was going to be okay."

Friendship

One of the most appealing threads running through *The Absolutely True Diary of a Part-Time Indian* is the friendship between Junior and Rowdy. They boys were born only hours apart, and they have been best friends ever since. Junior is awkward and weak and nerdy, and Rowdy is an angry bully; for each of them, their friendship is essential, because each has only one friend. However, these are adolescent boys, and they do not permit themselves to express their affection for each other directly. Instead, they insult each other, punch and wrestle each other, and exchange trash talk on the basketball court.

When Rowdy learns that Junior is transferring to Reardan, he cannot say that he will miss Junior or that he would be afraid to go. He cries, is ashamed of crying, and ends up punching Junior in the face. When Junior misses Rowdy at Thanksgiving, he shows his longing by drawing a cartoon of the two boys together and bringing it to Rowdy's house. Rowdy will not come to the door, will not admit that he likes the cartoon, and makes an obscene gesture at Junior, but Junior guesses from the fact that Rowdy does not tear up the cartoon that there is some lingering respect.

At the end of the novel, when Rowdy breaks

down and comes over to see Junior, he cannot admit that he misses his friend or that he admires his bravery. He says that he still hates Junior but has come over because "he's bored." When Rowdy yells "I hate you" and when Junior realizes that "my best friend had become my worst enemy," the reader knows that the friendship will endure, even if the boys do not dare believe it or show it. As the two friends play basketball in the final chapter, they come the closest they have ever come to having a heartfelt conversation, but Rowdy laces his sentimental talk with vulgarities and insults.

Family

Junior's relationship with his parents is a complicated one. On one level, it is straightforward and positive: he loves his parents, and they love him and each other. His parents do not hesitate in allowing him to transfer to Reardan High School, although it is twenty-two miles away and coming up with gas money is a struggle. They do their best to get him new clothes for school, to give him rides when they can, and to lend him a suit for the formal. Before Junior leaves for Reardan, Rowdy spends a lot of time at Junior's house because his own father is frequently drunk and violent, but Rowdy knows he is safe with Junior's parents. In addition to his parents, Junior has an older sister and a grandmother who are also positive influences, sharing advice and affection.

However, *The Absolutely True Diary of a Part-*

Time Indian is not a 1950s family television show, and Junior's family is not a model family. They are poor, and Junior reveals early on, "My mother and father are drunks." His mother does not drink much, but Junior's father is frequently drunk, and Junior knows that, although his dad means well, he cannot be relied on. Often his dad drives Junior to school, but sometimes he simply forgets or has spent all of the family's money on drinking. At Christmastime, Junior's dad "did what he always does when we don't have enough money. He took what little money we did have and ran away to get drunk." Mary, Junior's sister, is a smart woman who dreams of being a writer, but her own alcoholism and severe depression lead her to run away to get married, live in a trailer, stay unemployed, and die young. Eugene, "a good guy and like an uncle" to Junior, dies in a drunken fight with a friend, and Junior's beloved grandmother is killed by a drunk driver.

Junior begins his journey surrounded with his family's love, but he loses three members to death, and he knows that he will have to leave the others behind in order to "have a better life out in the white world." In the novel's second-to-last chapter, Junior and his parents go to the cemetery to clean the family graves. "I'm crazy about you," his father says, and his mother tells Junior, "I'm so proud of you." Alexie deliberately makes this the last look the reader has of Junior's family—a scene of love and pride and support.

Bildungsroman

The Absolutely True Diary of a Part-Time Indian is an example of a type of novel called a *bildungsroman*, or the "coming of age" novel. Typically, this kind of novel tells the story of a young person who moves from innocence to insight or from youth to maturity and who faces challenges and learns lessons along the way. Also, the character is typically pushed away from home out into the wider world early in the novel. Here the protagonist, Junior, leaves his home—or his feeling that he is home on the Spokane Indian Reservation—and heads out into a wealthy all-white town to find knowledge and experiences that would not otherwise be available to him. At first he is rejected by his new society, but he gradually acquires the skills he needs to be accepted and to succeed.

Junior's development begins with formal education. He realizes, with the help of Mr. P and his mother's old textbook, that he will never be able to get a decent high school education in his local school; in fact, he rejects two better schools on the reservation to select Reardan High School, the best school in the area. However, his education goes beyond school. He also learns that white people can be friends, that he is smart and capable, and that the only way he will ever realize his dreams—as his parents were never able to realize theirs—is to eventually leave the reservation forever behind him. This last lesson is a bittersweet one. As he watches his Reardan basketball team celebrating its win over the Wellpinit team, he realizes with sadness and shame that Rowdy and the others will never go to college, never succeed financially, and never escape the burden of alcoholism. Like many protagonists in the coming-of-age novel, Junior learns that, once he sets out on his journey, he can never go back.

Illustrations

Perhaps the most unusual element of *The Absolutely True Diary of a Part-Time Indian* is the inclusion of the illustrations by Ellen Forney. The protagonist, Junior, is constantly drawing cartoons that introduce the important people in his life or express his deepest, most complex feelings. As he puts it, "I draw because I want to talk to the world. And I want the world to pay attention to me. I feel important with a pen in my hand." As an adolescent with multiple disabilities, including a lisp and a stammer, Junior has found that he can express himself better with his pen than through speaking. When his best friend Rowdy refuses to speak to him, Junior makes his first approach by drawing a cartoon of the two boys together and delivering it to Rowdy.

There are sixty drawings in the novel, all of them ostensibly drawn by Junior; several of them are made to look as though they have been drawn on notebook paper, crumpled up in a backpack, smoothed out, and taped into the book. Junior includes drawings of his parents, his sister, his grandmother, his friend Rowdy, Eugene, Penelope, and others, labeled with their favorite clothing and most revealing possessions. Many of the drawings show Junior feeling lonely or nervous or embarrassed.

In an important cartoon in the chapter "How to Fight Monsters," drawn on Junior's first day at Reardan, he illustrates the feelings that give the novel its title: he shows a high school kid with a line drawn top to bottom down his middle. On one side, the kid is white, full of hope, with nice clothes and "a bright future"; on the other side he is Indian, with "bone-crushing reality" instead of hope, inexpensive clothes, and "a vanishing past." As time passes, Junior becomes more like the white kids and becomes like both sides of the drawing at once. He *becomes* a part-time Indian. Junior as narrator is not reticent about sharing his feelings in words with his readers, but Junior the character keeps most of his feelings to himself, expressing them mainly through his private drawings.

Native American Literature

Although Native American oral traditions reach back hundreds of years, it was not until the second half of the twentieth century that Native American authors began writing and publishing books that reached a large, mainstream readership. Many critics use the year 1968, the year that N. Scott Momaday's novel *House Made of Dawn* won the Pulitzer Prize, as the beginning of what they call the Native American Renaissance. Several events contributed to this Renaissance: the honorable service of many Native Americans in the Vietnam War, the success of the civil rights movement and the feminist movement, and an increased awareness among whites of Native American culture and social issues. James Ruppert, in "Fiction: 1968 to the Present," notes that this period was important for Native American writers, for "suddenly it seemed possible that they could be successful with their writing and still remain true to their unique experience."

Ruppert walks his readers through the decades after 1968. He notes that the 1970s produced writing that often reflected a romantic view of the past, celebrating the old ways and saving the old stories from being forgotten, and the 1980s brought a flourishing of Native American writers, including

Leslie Marmon Silko and Louise Erdrich, who reached large audiences and won major awards. He credits Erdrich, whose *Love Medicine* (1984) won the National Book Critics Circle Award for Fiction, with introducing humor.

By the time Alexie began publishing poetry and then fiction in the 1990s, there was already a place for Native American literature in the bookstores and the schools. One strand of this writing is exemplified by Joseph Bruchac, who has published several popular retellings of traditional tales, including the collection *Between Earth and Sky: Legends of Native American Sacred Places* (1996). Alexie and his contemporaries have attempted to write in a new voice and to explore what it means to be a Native American today. This new fiction is not set in a romantic past or out in the desert or the forest, but on the poverty-stricken, alcohol-and despair-filled reservation. As Ruppert writes, Alexie's "reservation dwellers do not contemplate myth or pronounce wisdom about nature."

Alexie is typical of Native American writers in the twenty-first century in his need to address two distinct audiences. In a 2007 interview with James Mellis, Alexie discussed his hope that *The Absolutely True Diary* would reach "a lot of native kids certainly, but also poor kids of any variety who feel trapped by circumstance, by culture, by low expectations." However, as he explains, a writer cannot make a living—or even find a publisher—by appealing only to poor children. Instead, he acknowledges that "college-educated white women" make up the largest share of book buyers, teachers, and librarians: "They seem to be the people who are most willing to ignore barriers and boundaries and to reach across, so that's who my audience is in reality." This need to be true to authentic experience while still appealing to a white readership has been a continual challenge and opportunity for Native American writers since the 1960s.

Through this period, even the terminology used by and for these writers has changed. "Native Americans" was used, beginning in the 1960s, as a polite and respectful term, and it was the term used by the federal government to take in all of the "native" groups, including Hawaiians. Later, many writers and activists, including Sherman Alexie, came to reject this bureaucratic term in favor of "Indian" or "American Indian." In the twenty-first century, many say that either term is acceptable, and "Native American" is the term used most in the classroom and in scholarship. Many individuals prefer to be labeled with the name of their tribe, rather than lumped together with other indigenous groups. Alexie is typically referred to by critics as a Coeur d'Alene/Spokane Indian, designating the tribes of which his father and mother were members, and Junior calls himself either a Spokane or an Indian.

Critical Overview

The Absolutely True Diary of a Part-Time Indian, Alexie's first book written for young-adult readers, was widely praised from its publication in 2007 and has become a popular book in schools and school libraries. It won dozens of awards, including the 2007 National Book Award for Young People's Literature, the 2008 American Indian Library Association American Indian Youth Literature Award, the 2008 *Boston Globe-Horn Book* Award for Excellence in Children's Literature in Fiction, and the 2008 Pacific Northwest Book Award. It was named to several "best books" lists in 2007, including those of the *New York Times, Los Angeles Times, School Library Journal, Horn Book, and Kirkus Reviews*.

Reviewers almost universally praised the book. Bruce Barcott, reviewing *The Absolutely True Diary for the New York Times*, notes that, although this was Alexie's first young-adult novel, "it took him only one book to master the form …. [T]his is a gem of a book." In the Minneapolis-St. Paul *Star Tribune*, Jim Lenfestey compares Alexie to J. D. Salinger and calls the novel "an absolutely honest, scary, and very funny bright light among the lost." *Los Angeles Times* contributor Susan Carpenter describes Alexie as a "masterful" writer who has been able "to transform sociological issues into a page turner that resonates with adolescent readers."

Many reviewers believe that the book could be helpful to young readers. Ian Chipman's review in *Booklist* comments that "younger teens looking for the strength to lift themselves out of rough situations would do well to start here." Writing for *Teenreads.com*, Jana Siciliano finds that "Junior's remarkable ability to weather even the worst possible storms ... makes this an uplifting yet very emotional reading experience."

The book has also been well-received outside the United States. Reviewing the novel for the London *Guardian*, Diane Samuels writes,

> Maybe it's the combination of drawings, pithy turns of phrase, candour, tragedy, despair and hope that makes this more than an entertaining read, more than an engaging story about a North American Indian kid who makes it out of a poor, dead-end background without losing his connection with who he is and where he's from.

She concludes that the novel is "humane, authentic and, most of all, it speaks." Beyond Great Britain, the novel has been published in twelve foreign editions.

Scholars have begun to examine the novel, as well, tying it to Alexie's earlier novels and short stories for adult readers and encouraging its use in classrooms. Jan Johnson, in an essay published in 2010, sees in *The Absolutely True Diary and in the novel Flight* (2007) that "empathy, compassion and forgiveness mark a possible way out of suffering and grief" and concludes that they "convey hopefulness not apparent earlier in Alexie's career." In a 2009 essay, Bryan Ripley Crandall recommends the novel for teachers of adolescents interested in issues of inclusion, arguing that "the story has the potential to promote discussions among a wide variety of students: those with disabilities, those who are seen as able, those from majority-dominant backgrounds, and those from minority cultures."

However, *The Absolutely True Diary* has not been universally admired. After a parent complaint about sexual references, the novel was removed from ninth grade English classes at Crook County High School in Prineville, Oregon, in 2008, and parents in Antioch, Illinois, tried to have the book removed from their local school's ninth grade summer reading list in 2009. In 2010, the book was officially banned from school classrooms in Stockton, Missouri. One of the school board members who voted in favor of the ban and who found the book offensive told Mike Penprase in the Springfield, Missouri *News-Leader*, "We can take the book and wrap it in those 20 awards everyone else said it won and it still is wrong." The novel was the second most frequently challenged book in schools and libraries in 2010, as listed by the American Library Association. The newsletter *Education Services News* listed the reasons for the challenges: "offensive language, racism, sex education, sexually explicit, unsuited to age group, violence."

Sources

Alexie, Sherman, *The Absolutely True Diary of a Part-Time Indian, Little*, Brown, 2007.

———, "Every Teen's Struggle: Speaking to a Universal Need," in *Publisher's Weekly*, Vol. 255, No. 7, February 18, 2008, p. 160.

Barcott, Bruce, "Off the Rez," in *New York Times*, November 11, 2007, http://www.nytimes.com/2007/11/11/books/review/I t.html (accessed March 30, 2011).

Carpenter, Susan, "Misfit," in *Los Angeles Times*, September 16, 2007, http://articles.latimes.com/2007/sep/16/books/bk-carpenter16 (accessed March 30, 2011).

Chipman, Ian, Review of *The Absolutely True Diary of a Part-Time Indian, in Booklist*, August 1, 2007.

Crandall, Bryan Ripley, "Adding a Disability Perspective When Reading Adolescent Literature: Sherman Alexie's *The Absolutely True Diary of a Part-Time Indian,"* in *ALAN Review*, Vol. 36, No. 2, Winter 2009, pp. 71–78.

Davis, Tanita, and Sarah Stevenson, "Sherman Alexie," in *Conversations with Sherman Alexie*, edited by Nancy J. Peterson, University of Mississippi Press, 2009, pp. 187–91.

Grassian, Daniel, "Understanding Sherman Alexie,"

in *Understanding Sherman Alexie*, University of South Carolina Press, 2005, pp. 1–14.

Guth, Amy, "Proposed Sherman Alexie Book-Ban in Suburban Chicago High School," in *Chicago Now*, June 22, 2009, http://www.chicagonow.com/blogs/chicago-subtext/2009/06/sherman-alexie-book-ban-antioch-chicago-suburban-high-school.html (accessed May 26, 2011).

Johnson, Jan, "Healing the Soul Wound in *Flight* and *The Absolutely True Diary of a Part-Time Indian*," in *Sherman Alexie: A Collection of Critical Essays*, University of Utah Press, 2010, pp. 224–40.

Lenfestey, Jim, "Straight Shooter," in *Star Tribune* (Minneapolis-St. Paul, MN), September 13, 2007, http://www.startribune.com/entertainment/books/11: (accessed March 30, 2011).

Mellis, James, "Interview with Sherman Alexie," in *Conversations with Sherman Alexie*, edited by Nancy J. Peterson, University of Mississippi Press, 2009, pp. 180–86.

Penprase, Mike, "Stockton Book Ban Upheld 7–0 in Packed Public Forum," in *News-Leader.com* (Springfield, MO), September 9, 2010, http://www.news-leader.com/article/20100909/NEWS04/9090375/Sto book-banupheld-7-0-in-packed-public-forum (accessed May 26, 2011).

"Prineville Board Bans Book after Parent Complains," in *KATU.com*, December 12, 2008,

http://www.katu.com/news/36051944.html
(accessed May 26, 2011).

Ruppert, James, "Fiction: 1968 to the Present," in *The Cambridge Companion to Native American Literature*, Cambridge University Press, 2005, pp. 173–88.

Samuels, Diane, "A Brave Life," in *Guardian* (London, England), October 4, 2008, http://www.guardian.co.uk/books/2008/oct/04/teena; (accessed May 3, 2011).

Siciliano, Jana, Review of *The Absolutely True Diary of a Part-Time Indian, in Teenreads.com*, http://www.teenreads.com/reviews/9780316013697. (accessed March 30, 2011).

"2010 ALA 'Banned Books List,'" in *Education Services News*, April 14, 2011, http://educationservicesnews.blogspot.com/2011/04/ala-banned-books-list.html (accessed May 26, 2011).

Further Reading

Banner, Stuart, *How the Indians Lost Their Land: Law and Power on the Frontier*, Belknap Press, 2005.

> This thorough and serious analysis by a law professor explains how the Europeans moved across North America, acquiring land and pushing the Native Americans ever westward. Although the book is detailed and tells a complex story, it is written in clear language for general readers.

Berglund, Jeff, and Jan Roush, eds., *Sherman Alexie: A Collection of Critical Essays*, University of Utah Press, 2010.

> This volume gathers fourteen critical essays about Alexie's fiction, poetry, and films. While a few of the pieces are rather technical, Berglund's introduction, Jan Johnson's essay on *Flight and The Absolutely True Diary*, and Angelica Lawson's analysis of gender roles in *Smoke Signals* offer interesting insights for general readers. The book also includes an extensive bibliography of primary and secondary sources.

Bruce, Heather E., Anna E. Baldwin, and Christabel

Umphrey, *Sherman Alexie in the Classroom*, National Council of Teachers of English, 2008.

> Part of the National Council of Teachers of English High School Literature Series, this volume provides ideas for teaching Alexie's films, short stories, poems, and novels. The chapter on *The Absolutely True Diary* and the novel *Flight* emphasizes Alexie's determination not to shield young people from the real world and the need to teach students about "understanding, reconciliation, responsibility" in a post-9/11 world.

Mihesuah, Devon A., *American Indians: Stereotypes and Realities*, Clarity Press, 2009.

> In an easy-to-follow two-part format, this book presents twenty-five common stereotypes about Indians, each followed by images, texts, and explanations that show why the stereotype is false. Also included is a list of "do's and don'ts for those who teach American Indian history and culture."

Moore, David L., "Sherman Alexie: Irony, Intimacy, and Agency," in *The Cambridge Companion to Native American Literature*, edited by Joy Porter and Kenneth M. Roemer, Cambridge University Press, 2005, pp. 297–310.

Published before *The Absolutely True Diary of a Part-Time Indian*, Moore's essay is a critical overview of Alexie's poetry, fiction, nonfiction, and film, placing his work in the larger context of Native American writing since 1968. Moore identifies several topics and themes —including identity racial tension, absent fathers, and basketball—that also inform *The Absolutely True Diary*.

Truer, David, *Native American Fiction: A User's Manual*, Graywolf Press, 2006.

In this collection of essays, novelist Truer suggests ways to read Native American fiction purely for its literary qualities rather than as historical or cultural artifacts. He analyzes works by several authors, including Leslie Marmon Silko and Louise Erdrich, and includes Alexie's *Indian Killer and Reservation Blues*.

Suggested Search Terms

Sherman Alexie

The Absolutely True Diary of a Part-Time Indian Native American literature Sherman Alexie AND diary

Sherman Alexie AND award

Sherman Alexie AND challenged books Sherman Alexie AND coming-of-age Sherman Alexie AND bildungsroman Sherman Alexie AND Native American literature Spokane Indians

Spokane Indians AND Sherman Alexie banned books AND The Absolutely True Diary of a Part-Time Indian The Absolutely True Diary of a Part-Time Indian AND controversy